DISASTERS IN HISTORY

THE GREAT SAN FRANCISCO

EARTHQUAKE AND FIRE

by Michael Burgan
illustrated by Phil Miller and
Charles Barnett III

Consultant:
Alison Moore
North Baker Research Library
California Historical Society
San Francisco, California

Capstone
press
Mankato, Minnesota

Graphic Library is published by Capstone Press,
151 Good Counsel Drive, P.O. Box 669, Mankato, Minnesota 56002.
www.capstonepress.com

1 2 3 4 5 6 12 11 10 09 08 07

Library of Congress Cataloging-in-Publication Data
Burgan, Michael.
    The great San Francisco Earthquake and fire / by Michael Burgan.
    p. cm.—(Graphic library. Disasters in history)
    Summary: "In graphic novel format, tells the story of the great San Francisco
Earthquake of 1906 and the subsequent fires"—Provided by publisher.
    Includes bibliographical references and index.
    ISBN-13: 978-1-4296-0155-9 (hardcover)
    ISBN-10: 1-4296-0155-8 (hardcover)
    1. San Francisco Earthquake, Calif., 1906—Comic books, strips, etc.—Juvenile
literature. 2. Earthquakes—California—San Francisco—History—20th century—Comic
books, strips, etc.—Juvenile literature. 3. Fires—California—San Francisco—History—20th
century—Comic books, strips, etc.—Juvenile literature. 4. San Francisco (Calif.)—History—
20th century—Comic books, strips, etc.—Juvenile literature. 5. Graphic novels. I. Title. II.
Series.
F869.S357B87 2008
979.4'61051
[2 22]   2007014929

Designers
Thomas Emery and Alison Thiele

Colorist
Matt Webb

Editors
Donald Lemke and Megan Schoeneberger

Editor's note: Direct quotations from primary sources are indicated by a yellow background.

Direct quotations appear on the following pages:
Page 9, from "The Great Quake 1906–2006: Days Before the Disaster," by Carl Nolte,
    San Francisco Chronicle (http://www.sfgate.com/cgi-bin/article.cgi?f=/c/a/2006/04/09/
    BAGQ09QUAKE.DTL&hw=days+before+the+disaster&sn=001&sc=1000).
Pages 15, 17, 19, from *The Great Earthquake and Firestorms of 1906: How San Francisco
    Nearly Destroyed Itself* by Philip L. Fradkin (Berkeley, Calif.: University of California
    Press, 2005).
Page 25, from "Timeline of the San Francisco Earthquake April 18–23, 1906." The Virtual
    Museum of the City of San Francisco (http://www.sfmuseum.net/hist10/06timeline.html).

TABLE OF CONTENTS

CHAPTER 1

GRAND CITY OF THE WEST

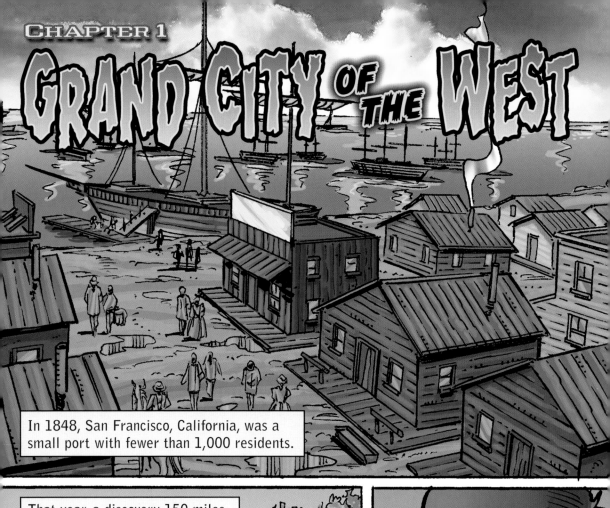

In 1848, San Francisco, California, was a small port with fewer than 1,000 residents.

That year, a discovery 150 miles (241 kilometers) east of the town changed its history forever.

Now what's this . . .

Gold!!

CHAPTER 4

A NEW SAN FRANCISCO

After the fire, about 250,000 people were left homeless. Many of the refugees gathered in Golden Gate Park, where they ate donated food.

What is it?

Lots of potatoes, lots of grain, and a little meat. We call it "earthquake stew."

By 1915, the rebuilding was finished. The city hosted a world's fair called the Panama Pacific International Exposition.

This fair shows everyone that San Francisco is a world-class city again.

You would never know there had ever been such terrible fires.

MORE ABOUT THE EARTHQUAKE AND FIRE

The earthquake lasted between 45 seconds and one minute. The strongest aftershock came at about 8:15 in the morning on April 18 and lasted for about 10 seconds.

The disaster destroyed more than 28,000 buildings in an area of about 4 square miles (10 square kilometers). The number of people who died was first thought to be about 500. Today, historians believe at least 3,000 people died in the disaster.

San Francisco was not the only city affected by the 1906 earthquake. In San Jose, south of San Francisco, the quake destroyed buildings and started fires. Firefighters there had enough water to quickly put out those fires. North of San Francisco, the city of Santa Rosa also had heavy damage. The quake was felt as far away as southern Oregon and central Nevada.

In 1907, James Phelan traveled across the United States. He told Americans that it was safe to do business in San Francisco. In 1913, he was elected to the U.S. Senate from the state of California.

Today, the fire hydrant used to put out the fire in the Mission District is called the Golden Hydrant. Each year on April 18, city residents paint the hydrant gold, to honor the role it played in stopping one of the major fires of 1906.

 A layer of the earth called the crust lies just below the land and oceans. The crust is made up of large and small regions called plates. Earthquakes occur along areas where two plates rub up against each other, called a fault. The movement of the plates along the fault—such as the San Andreas Fault in California—creates an earthquake.

 Scientists who study earthquakes are seismologists. They use a system called the Richter scale to measure the power of earthquakes. The scale goes from 1 to 8.8. An earthquake that measures a 7 is one million times stronger than one that measures a 1. The Richter scale was invented after the 1906 quake, but scientists think it would have been measured at about 7.9, making it one of the most powerful earthquakes ever recorded.

 Some seismologists who work for the U.S. government think there is a strong chance another major quake will hit San Francisco before 2031.

GLOSSARY

blasting cap (BLAST-ing KAP)—a small explosive that is used to blow up larger explosives, such as dynamite

explosive (ek-SPLOH-siv)—a chemical that can blow up

guncotton (GUHN-kot-uhn)—a kind of material that easily catches fire

loot (LOOT)—to steal from stores or houses during wartime or after a disaster

refugee (ref-yuh-JEE)—a person forced to flee his or her home because of natural disaster or war

reservoir (REZ-ur-vwar)—a holding area for large amounts of water

INTERNET SITES

FactHound offers a safe, fun way to find Internet sites related to this book. All of the sites on FactHound have been researched by our staff.

Here's how:
1. Visit *www.facthound.com*
2. Choose your grade level.
3. Type in this book ID **1429601558** for age-appropriate sites. You may also browse subjects by clicking on letters, or by clicking on pictures and words.
4. Click on the **Fetch It** button.

FactHound will fetch the best sites for you!

READ MORE

Cooke, Tim. *1906 San Francisco Earthquake.* Disasters. Milwaukee: Gareth Stevens, 2005.

Nobleman, Marc Tyler. *The San Francisco Earthquake of 1906.* We the People. Minneapolis: Compass Point Books, 2007.

Tanaka, Shelley. *Earthquake!: On a Peaceful Spring Morning Disaster Strikes San Francisco.* A Day That Changed America. New York: Hyperion Books for Children, 2004.

Worth, Richard. *The San Francisco Earthquake.* Environmental Disasters. New York: Facts on File, 2005.

BIBLIOGRAPHY

Fradkin, Philip L. *The Great Earthquake and Firestorms of 1906: How San Francisco Nearly Destroyed Itself.* Berkeley, Calif.: University of California Press, 2005.

Morris, Charles. *The San Francisco Calamity by Earthquake and Fire.* Urbana, Ill.: University of Illinois Press, 2002.

Smith, Dennis. *San Francisco Is Burning: The Untold Story of the 1906 Earthquake and Fires.* New York: Viking, 2005.

Winchester, Simon. *A Crack in the Edge of the World: America and the Great California Earthquake of 1906.* New York: HarperCollins, 2005.

INDEX